IRELAND

teNeues

IRELAND

Photographs by Wolfgang Fritz
Text by Michael Scott

teNeues

Ireland is a feast for the eyes and for the spirit. For more than six thousand years, this island set like a jewel at the edge of the Atlantic has been inhabited by people who appreciated its special qualities, both physical and spiritual.

Here is a place where the past is more than palpable. The past is woven in the fabric of the society, it can be seen, touched, climbed upon, explored and experienced. Glens, mountains and valleys are peopled with memories that will not die, the ancient streets of the cities are touched by the spirits of its turbulent history.

The island of Ireland consists of a low lying central plain bordered by mountains on both coasts, overlooking the sea. Warmed by the Gulf Stream, it enjoys a mild climate and high rainfall. This rainfall has helped to sculpt a land composed of Pleistocene deposits above a base of Paleozoic rock. The stone of the mountains, the cliffs, the eroded rock that erupts through grass and moss makes Ireland a symphony of green and gray.

Like the people, the stones have character. The soft limestone of County Clare reminds one of the gentle voices of its people. The lines of the granite mountains of Donegal are echoed in the strong faces of its men, and are as enduring as legends of the great heroic figures of Red Hugh O'Donnell, Cuchulain and Brian Boru.

The stones of Ireland vary from the glittering quartzite of Croagh Patrick, the holy mountain in Mayo that was home to the nation's Patron Saint, to the weird and unique basaltic cylinders of the Giant's Causeway in County Antrim. From such materials, monuments of enduring mystery have been created.

The architecture of the country owes a lot to its Christian past: this is a land of monasteries and cathedrals, of churches and abbeys. The sometimes troubled relationship with England has also left its mark on the landscape: here is land of castles and towers and, in the cities, of sweeping architectural masterpieces, of grandiose houses and impressive streets.

This country has inspired generations of scholars and writers, of painters, poets and playwrights. Swift, Yeats and Synge, Joyce, Beckett and Heaney: their work, so solidly grounded in the country of their birthplace, enjoys an international reputation. For its size, no other country in the world has produced so many poets and writers.

Ireland is however, a country of contrasts. The old and the new sit, sometimes uneasily, side-by-side. The cities are beginning to encroach into the countryside. The thriving Celtic Tiger economy, inexorably associated with the European Union, established a new and dynamic culture. The country boasts one of the youngest populations in Europe and the capital, Dublin, is a thoroughly modern European city, with its newfound wealth visible on every corner.

However, only a few miles away, the wind blows across the ancient Hill of Tara as it has done since before the dawn of history, and sheep graze on the grass where once walked the Magic People, the Tuatha De Danann.

Ireland may be changing, but its heart, its soul, is eternal.

Michael Scott

Irland – das ist ein Fest für Sinne und Seele. Seit über 6000 Jahren wissen die Menschen auf dieser Insel, die wie ein grün schimmerndes Juwel im Atlantik liegt, ihre landschaftlichen und spirituellen Eigenheiten zu schätzen.

Die Vergangenheit ist hier allenthalben greifbar. Sie ist in die Gesellschaft eingewoben, man kann sie sehen, berühren, auf ihr herumklettern, sie erforschen und erleben. In den Bergen, Schluchten und Tälern überdauern unauslöschliche Erinnerungen, und in den Straßen der alten Städte lebt der Geist der wechselvollen irischen Geschichte fort.

Im Innern der Insel erstreckt sich eine Ebene, die zu beiden Küsten hin von Bergen gesäumt ist. Dank des warmen Golfstroms ist das Klima mild und niederschlagsreich. Der Regen hat die Ablagerungen aus dem Pleistozän, die über einer Felsschicht aus dem Paläozoikum liegen, charakteristisch geformt. Der Fels der Berge, die Klippen, das erodierte Gestein, das durch Gras und Moos stößt, fügen sich in Irland zu einer Sinfonie aus Grün- und Grautönen zusammen.

Wie die Menschen, so haben auch die Steine Charakter. Der weiche Kalk des County Clare erinnert an die sanften Stimmen seiner Bewohner, die Konturen der Granitberge von Donegal spiegeln sich in den ausdrucksvollen Gesichtern der Männer wider. Die Steine sind so beständig wie die Legenden der großen Nationalhelden Red Hugh O'Donnell, Cuchulain und Brian Boru.

Die Palette des irischen Gesteins reicht vom glitzernden Quarz des Croagh Patrick, dem heiligen Berg in Mayo und Heimat des Schutzpatrons Irlands, bis hin zu den bizarren Basaltzylindern des Giant's Causeway in County Antrim. Solches Gestein hat Landmarken hervorgebracht, die in ihrer Rätselhaftigkeit die Zeit überdauern.

Die Architektur Irlands ist von seiner christlichen Vergangenheit geprägt: Dies ist das Land der Kathedralen, Kirchen und Klöster. Auch das bisweilen schwierige Verhältnis zu England hat dem Land seinen Stempel aufgedrückt: Landauf landab erheben sich stolze Burgen und Herrenhäuser, in den Städten sind architektonische Meisterwerke, prächtige Häuser und eindrucksvolle Straßen zu bewundern.

Das Land hat Generationen von Gelehrten und Schriftstellern, Malern, Dichtern und Dramatikern inspiriert. Swift, Yeats und Synge, Joyce, Beckett und Heaney: Ihre Arbeit, fest in der Erde ihrer Heimat verankert, genießt internationales Ansehen. Gemessen an seiner Größe, hat kein Land der Erde so viele Schriftsteller hervorgebracht.

Doch Irland ist auch ein Land der Gegensätze. Das Alte und das Neue stehen bisweilen unbehaglich Seite an Seite. Die Städte breiten sich immer weiter ins Umland aus. Und mit der florierenden Wirtschaft des keltischen Tigers, die untrennbar mit der Europäischen Union verbunden ist, hat eine neue, dynamische Kultur Einzug gehalten. Die irische Bevölkerung ist eine der jüngsten Europas, die Hauptstadt Dublin eine durch und durch moderne europäische Stadt, deren neu erworbener Reichtum überall spürbar ist.

Doch nur wenige Kilometer entfernt bläst der Wind über die alten Hügel von Tara, wie er es seit Menschengedenken getan hat. Schafe grasen dort, wo vor langer Zeit das sagenumwobene Volk der Tuatha De Danann lebte.

Irland mag im Wandel begriffen sein, doch sein Herz, seine Seele währen ewig.

Michael Scott

L'Irlande – une fête pour les sens et pour l'âme. Depuis plus de 6000 ans, les gens de cette île, qui se trouve comme un joyau vert brillant dans l'Atlantique, savent apprécier les particularités de son paysage et spirituelles.

Ici, le passé se ressent partout. Il est intégré dans la société, on peut le voir, le toucher, grimper dessus, l'étudier et le vivre. Dans les montagnes, les gorges et les vallées, des souvenirs impérissables survivent et, dans les rues des vieilles villes, l'esprit de l'histoire irlandaise mouvementée est encore vivant.

A l'intérieur de l'île s'étire une plaine bordée sur les deux côtes par des montagnes. Grâce au Gulf Stream chaud, le climat est doux et pluvieux. La pluie a formé de façon caractéristique les dépôts du Pléistocène qui se trouvent au-dessus d'une couche de roche du Paléozoïque. La roche des montagnes, les brisants, la pierre érodée qui traverse l'herbe et la mousse, s'unissent en Irlande pour créer une symphonie de verts et de gris.

Tout comme les hommes, les pierres ont également leur caractère. La craie molle du County Clare rappelle les voix douces de ses habitants, les contours des montagnes de granite de Donegal se reflètent dans les visages expressifs des hommes. Les pierres sont aussi constantes que les légendes des grands héros nationaux Red Hugh O'Donnell, Cuchulain et Brian Boru.

La diversité de la pierre irlandaise va du quartz brillant du Croagh Patrick, la montagne sacrée de Mayo et la patrie du saint patron de l'Irlande, aux bizarres cylindres de basalte du Giant's Causeway à County Antrim. De telles pierres ont généré des marques dans le paysage qui, dans leur énigme, survivent au temps.

L'architecture de l'Irlande est empreinte du passé chrétien : C'est le pays des cathédrales, des églises et des cloîtres. Et la relation parfois difficile avec l'Angleterre a également imprimé son sceau sur le pays : Dans tout le pays, il existe de fiers châteaux et maisons de maîtres, dans les villes, l'on peut admirer des chefs-d'œuvre architecturaux, de magnifiques maisons et des rues impressionnantes.

Le pays a inspiré des générations de savants et d'écrivains, de peintres, poètes et dramaturges. Swift, Yeats et Synge, Joyce, Beckett et Heaney : Leur travail, bien ancré dans la terre de leur patrie, jouit d'une renommée internationale. Comparé à sa grandeur, aucun pays du monde n'a vu naître autant d'écrivains.

Mais l'Irlande est aussi un pays des contraires. Le vieux et le nouveau se trouvent parfois côte à côte de manière inconfortable. Les villes s'étendent de plus en plus. Et, avec l'économie florissante du tigre celte, liée de façon indissoluble à l'Union Européenne, une nouvelle culture dynamique a fait son apparition. La population irlandaise est l'une des plus jeunes d'Europe, la capitale Dublin est une ville européenne absolument moderne, dont la nouvelle richesse se ressent partout.

Mais, à quelques kilomètres seulement, le vent souffle sur les vieilles collines de Tara, tel qu'il le fait depuis toujours. Des moutons paissent là où vivait, il y a longtemps, le peuple légendaire de la Tuatha De Danann.

L'Irlande est peut-être en train de changer, mais son cœur et son âme sont éternels.

Michael Scott

Irlanda es una fiesta para la cabeza y el alma. Desde hace más de 6.000 años la gente de esta isla, que es como una joya verde y resplandeciente en mitad del Atlántico, sabe valorar sus particularidades paisajísticas y espirituales.

El pasado está al alcance por todas partes. Está enlazado con la sociedad; uno puede verlo, tocarlo, trepar encima de él, explorarlo y vivirlo. Recuerdos imborrables persisten en los montes, en los barrancos y los valles y, en las calles de las antiguas ciudades continúa aquel espíritu de esa variada historia irlandesa.

En el interior de la isla se extiende una llanura que hacia los dos litorales está rodeada de montañas. Gracias al aire cálido del golfo el clima es suave con muchas precipitaciones. La lluvia ha dado una forma característica a los sedimentos del Pleistoceno que están situados encima de una capa rocosa de Paleozoico. Las rocas de las montañas, las peñas, el mineral erosionado, rodeado de hierba y musgo, componen una sinfonía de tonos verdes y grises.

Al igual que las personas, también las piedras tienen su carácter. La cal suave del County Clare hace recordar esas voces tiernas de sus habitantes, los contornos de las montañas de granito de Donegal se reflejan en los rostros expresivos de los hombres. Las piedras son tan persistentes como las leyendas de los grandes héroes nacionales Red Hugh O'Donnell, Cuchulain y Brian Boru.

La paleta de minerales irlandeses llega desde el cuarzo brillante del Croagh Patrick, la montaña santa situada en Mayo y tierra del patrón de Irlanda, hasta los cilindros de basalto del Giant's Causeway en County Antrim. Este mineral ha engendrado comarcas que sobreviven a los tiempos por su carácter enigmático.

La arquitectura de Irlanda está marcada por su pasado cristiano. Es el país de las catedrales, iglesias y monasterios. También su a veces difícil relación con Inglaterra a imprimido su carácter a este país. Hacia el norte como hacia el sur del país se elevan fortalezas y caseríos llenos de orgullo, en las ciudades se pueden admirar obras maestras de la arquitectura, grandiosas casas y calles imponentes.

Este país ha inspirado a generaciones de eruditos y escritores, de pintores, poetas y dramaturgos. Swift, Yeats y Synge, Joyce, Beckett y Heaney: su trabajo, liado fuertemente a su tierra, goza de prestigio internacional. En comparación con su extensión, ningún país del mundo ha producido tantos escritores.

Pero, Irlanda es también el país de los contrastes. Lo antiguo y lo moderno viven puerta con puerta, a veces en una manera incómoda para ambos. Las ciudades se expanden cada vez más hacia sus inmediaciones. Y, con la economía próspera del tigre celta, inseparablemente ligada a la Unión Europea, ha llegado la hora de una cultura nueva y dinámica. La población irlandesa es una de las más jóvenes de Europa y la capital Dublín es de parte a parte una moderna ciudad europea cuya nueva riqueza se puede percibir en todos sus rincones.

Pero a sólo unos pocos kilómetros el viento sopla por encima de las antiguas colinas de Tara de la misma manera que lo ha hecho desde tiempos inmemoriales. Ahora las ovejas pacen allá, dónde hace largo tiempo el pueblo de los Tuatha De Danann vivía, cubierto de leyendas.

Posiblemente Irlanda esté cambiando, pero su corazón y su alma perdurarán eternamente.

Michael Scott

L'Irlanda –è una festa per i sensi e l'anima. Da oltre 6000 anni gli uomini di quest'isola, che risplende nell'Atlantico come uno smeraldo, sanno apprezzare le peculiarità paesaggistiche e spirituali.

Il passato qui è tangibile ovunque. È intessuto nella società, lo si può vedere, toccare, scalare, esplorare e sperimentare. Su monti, dirupi e valli sopravvivono ricordi indelebili, e nelle vie delle città antiche, continua a vivere lo spirito della multiforme storia irlandese.

All'interno dell'isola si estende una pianura, fiancheggiata dai monti fino ad entrambe le coste. Grazie alla corrente calda del golfo, il clima è mite e ricco di precipitazioni. La pioggia ha conferito una forma caratteristica alle sedimentazioni del pleistocene, che si trovano su di uno strato di roccia del paleozoico. La roccia delle montagne, le scogliere, la roccia erosa, che s'imbatte in erba e muschio, in Irlanda si combinano in una sinfonia di toni verdi e grigi.

Come gli uomini, anche le pietre hanno un carattere. La calce tenera di County Clare ricorda le voci sommesse dei suoi abitanti, i contorni della montagna di granito di Donegal si rispecchiano nei volti espressivi degli uomini. Le pietre sono così durevoli, come le leggende dei grandi eroi nazionali Red Hugh O'Donnell, Cuchulain e Brian Boru.

La varietà di roccia irlandese va dal quarzo scintillante di Croagh Patrick, la montagna sacra di Mayo e patria del patrono, dell'Irlanda, fino ai bizzarri cilindri di basalto del Giant's Causeway nella County Antrim. Tale roccia ha prodotto punti di riferimento che, nella loro natura enigmatica, sopravvivono al tempo.

L'architettura dell'Irlanda è intrisa del suo passato cristiano: è la terra delle cattedrali, delle chiese e dei monasteri. Anche il di tanto in tanto difficile rapporto con l'Inghilterra ha dato la propria impronta al paese: per tutto il paese si ergono con orgoglio roccaforti e case signorili, nelle città si ammirano capolavori architettonici, case sontuose e strade imponenti.

Questo paese ha ispirato generazioni di studiosi e scrittori, pittori, poeti e drammaturghi. Swift, Yeats e Synge, Joyce, Beckett e Heaney: la loro opera, ancorata saldamente alla terra della loro patria, ha considerazione internazionale. Comparato alla sua grandezza, nessun paese al mondo ha prodotto così tanti scrittori.

Ma l'Irlanda è anche il paese delle contraddizioni. Il vecchio e il nuovo di tanto in tanto stanno fianco a fianco sgradevolmente. Le città si distendono sempre fino ai dintorni. E con l'economia fiorente della tigre celtica, unita inseparabilmente all'Unione Europea, ha fatto ingresso una nuova cultura dinamica. Il popolo irlandese è il più giovane d'Europa, la capitale Dublino è da capo a piedi una moderna città europea, la cui ricchezza recentemente acquisita è dovunque percepibile.

Solo a pochi chilometri di distanza il vento soffia sulle antiche colline di Tara, come ha fatto a memoria d'uomo. Le pecore pascolano laddove tanto tempo fa visse il leggendario popolo di Tuatha De Danann.

L'Irlanda può darsi che si stia trasformando, ma il suo cuore e la sua anima durano in eterno.

Michael Scott

72

Brian
Og

IRISH
IRISH

THE
LORD
EDWARD
PL TEAMPAILL CRIOST
CHRISTCHURCH PLACE
23
T. CUNNIAM
23

SPIRITS
149
The Boar's Head

SHAWS

WD125
D20

30

PREMIUM BEER
HARP
LAGER
NATURALLY BREWED

THE CELLAR
Estd. 1986
DRINKING EMPORIUM
ESTD 1759
GUINNES
WINES
HANRAHAN'S
SPIRITS
Purbeyors
of
Finest
Drinks
from
Grape
and
Grain

GUINNESS

The Atlantic Inn
THE GAFF
JILL II
CORK

COUNTING
HOUSE

ROYAL LIVER
ASSURANCE
The People's Choice
CARLING BLACK LABEL LAGER
Carlsberg
Carlsberg
CORK DOMESTIC
APPLIANCES LTD
IRISH FERRIES

ALLEGRO
ESTAURANT
DUGGS
CAFÉ
estb. 1869
traditional
PUB
ITALIAN
KILLARNEY
FIRE & SECURITY
PAINTINGS
PRINTS
ENGRAVINGS
The Killarney Art Gallery
LYONS TEA
SOLD HERE
"CAPSTAN" NAVY CUT
TOBACCO & CIGARETTES
ART Gallery
Fine Irish PAINTINGS
ART Gallery
Artists supplies
Antique prints & Engravings
golf, hunting etc
ART Gallery
Oil Paintings Cleaned and Restored

THE
BOOK

OVENS
REPAIRED & REBODIED
12 McINERNEY & SONS 12
CANDLEMAKER
SHERRY

JOHNNY PATTERSON
1860 1889
ORIGINAL IRISH CLOWN
Foodstore
GUERIN'S
Newsagency
Golden Vale
FRESH
Milk
IRISH

Directory Verzeichnis Table des matières Directorio Indice delle materie

Bloody Forelanc
The
Glencolumkille
Slieve League
Teelin Bay
Benbulb
Achill Island
Newport
Westport
IRE
Ashford Castle
Kylemore Abbey
Ross Abbey
Dunmore
Connemara
National Park
Lough Corrib
Doolin
The Burren
Cliffs of Moher
Kilfenora
Ennis
Quin
Bunratty Castle and Folk P
Limerick
Adare
Listowel
Croom
Tralee
Dingle
Killarney
Lough Leane
Glanworth
Cork
Ring of Kerry
Kenmare
Sneem

Giant's
Causeway
Portrush
Dunluce Castle
Doe Castle
Glenveagh
National Park
rkenny
NORTHERN
IRELAND
Monasterboice
Mellifont Abbey
Trim
Bective
Skerries
Lusk
acnoise
Dublin
Powerscourt
Wicklow Mountains
Kilkenny
Rock of Cashel
Jerpoint Abbey
New Ross
Cahir
Wexford
Waterford
Johnstown
Castle
lelleray
Dunmore East
Ardmore

Front cover: Cliffs of Moher
Back cover: Near Listowel / Doe Castle / Dublin / Dunmore East

Prof. Wolfgang Fritz
Foto-Design
Bugenhagenstr. 17
51061 Köln
Tel. 0049-(0) 221-646782
Fax. 0049-(0) 221-644505

Photographs by Wolfgang Fritz
Design by Iris Durie
Introduction by Michael Scott
Translations by
Dr. Anne Emmert, Creglingen (German)
Danielle Deweerdt, ASCO International (French)
José Álvarez, ASCO International (Spanish)
Bruna D'Elia, ASCO International (Italian)
English translation of the back cover text by
Killian Nolan, ASCO International
Editorial coordination by Sabine Scholz
Production by Sandra Jansen
Color separation by Medien Team-Vreden, Germany

Bibliographic information published by Die Deutsche Bibliothek. Die Deutsche Bibliothek lists this publication in the Deutsche Nationalbibliographie; detailed bibliographic data is available in the Internet at http://dnb.ddb.de

ISBN 3-8237-9001-2

Printed in Italy

teNeues Publishing Group
Kempen
Düsseldorf
London
Madrid
New York
Paris

Published by teNeues Publishing Group

teNeues Book Division
Kaistraße 18
40221 Düsseldorf
Germany
Phone: 0049-(0)211-99 45 97-0
Fax: 0049-(0)211-99 45 97-40
e-mail: books@teneues.de
Press department: arehn@teneues.de
Phone: 0049-(0)2152-916-202

teNeues Publishing Company
16 West 22nd Street
New York, N.Y. 10010
USA
Phone: 001-212-627-9090
Fax: 001-212-627-9511

teNeues Publishing UK Ltd.
P.O. Box 402
West Byfleet
KT14 7ZF
Great Britain
Phone: 0044-1932-403509
Fax: 0044-1932-403514

teNeues France S.A.R.L.
4, rue de Valence
75005 Paris
France
Phone: 0033-1-55 76 62 05
Fax: 0033-1-55 76 64 19

www.teneues.com

Published in the same series:

GREECE	3-8327-9002-0
PROVENCE	3-8238-4575-6
TOSCANA	3-8238-4567-5

teNeues